مواعظ الإمام أحمد بن حنبل

Advice and Admonitions: Imām Aḥmad b. Ḥanbal
First Edition
Published by Ark of Knowledge Publications, Leeds
info@aokpubs.com

ISBN: 9798854865036

Cover design and typesetting by ihsaandesign.com.

Printed by Amazon KDP

مواعظ الإمام أحمد بن حنبل

ADVICE and ADMONITIONS

Imām Aḥmad b. Ḥanbal

A Translation of
Mawāʿiẓ al-Imām Aḥmad bin Ḥanbal

Compiled by Ṣāliḥ Aḥmad ash-Shāmī

Translated by Dr Azhar Majothi

Edited and Annotated by Abū Ubaydah Arsalān Yūnus

Ark of Knowledge
PUBLICATIONS

Contents

LESSONS IN PATIENCE AND FORTITUDE

Publisher's Note

I begin with every beautiful name that belongs to Allāh, the Most Gracious, the Most Merciful.

All complete praise is due to Allāh alone the *Rabb*[1] of all that exists. May blessings and greetings be upon the best of His creation Muḥammad, the last and final Messenger, and upon his family, companions and all those who follow him until the day of Judgement.

This is a comprehensive translation of some of the admonitions and words of advice by the great Imām, Aḥmad b. Ḥanbal compiled by Shaykh Ṣāliḥ ash-Shāmī, the first of many works I hope to publish under Ark of Knowledge Publications.

Some beneficial footnotes have been added by the translator and marked [TN]; I have added a short biography of the Imām and further points of benefit which are marked [EN] to aid the reader in understanding the Imām's intended meaning at various points.

Although every effort has been made to ensure this modern translation is as accurate as possible, if there are any obvious errors in it, then I would be deeply grateful to its readers to provide feedback and guidance.

I hope that this book benefits others. If so, then it is only a blessing from Allāh, and then the product of guidance from my teachers and encouragement of sincere friends. I also hope that with works like this, I can make a modest contribution to the right understanding of Islam. I sincerely ask Allāh to accept my meagre efforts in this regard.

I ask Allāh to make this simple endeavour a source of pleasure for us all and a source of success in the Hereafter. *Āmīn.*

Abū Ubaydah Arsalān Yūnus
Muḥarram, 1445

---

1. [TN] The word *Rabb* has a vast meaning. Its detailed meaning is the Sustainer, Cherisher, Master and Nourisher.

Biography
Imām Aḥmad b. Ḥanbal (164-241 A.H.)

Name
His name was Aḥmad b. Mohammad b. Hanbal ash-Shaybani and his Kunyah was Abū ʾAbdullāh. His tribe was Shayban which was known for courage and chivalry.

His father was a soldier stationed at Khurasan and died young at the age of 30 when Imām Aḥmad was only 3 years old. Imām Aḥmad is typically associated with his grandfather so it is said, Aḥmad b. Hanbal because his grandfather (Hanbal) was more known than his father. His mother's name was Sāfīyah bint Maymunah who was also from the same tribe of Shayban. She took care of him and brought him up in the most proper manner as she was keen that he learnt the different disciplines of knowledge prevalent at that time.

His Birth And Upbringing
Imām Aḥmad was born and raised in Baghdad, Iraq. He was born in the year 164 Hijrī corresponding to the year 780 AD. He was a scribe at a young age and was known for his politeness as well as his good manners. He was not a boy who spent his childhood in frivolous pursuits rather he was a complete mature [minded] adult despite his young age.

Seeking Knowledge
Imām Aḥmad started his education in Baghdad and sought knowledge of ḥadīth form Hushaim b. Bashīr. Subsequently he travelled to Makkah, Madinah, Kufa, Basrah and Yemen to gain knowledge from different scholars. During his travels he wrote down around 300,000 Aḥādīth. He learned and wrote Aḥādīth from more than 300 scholars.

He performed Hajj 5 times, 3 of them times were being on foot.

Imām Aḥmad said, "I will seek knowledge until I enter the grave."

His Virtues

Imām Ibn Hibbān said in his book *ath-Thiqat,* vol.8, p.18-19 that,

> He [Imām Aḥmad] was a *Ḥāfiẓ*, excellent, pious, *Faqīh*. He strictly abode by observing the religion with zeal, without disclosure and never ending worship. Allāh helped the Ummah of Muḥammad (ﷺ) through him. This is [true] by [the fact] that he remained firm in times of trial, devoted himself to Allāh and was ready to be martyred. He was beaten by stones, Allāh saved him from disbelief and made him a person worth following. He was such a shelter that people used to find shelter under him.

Imām Abū Hatim said in his book *al-Jarh wa 't-Ta'dil,* vol.1 pg.302 that,"When you see a man loving Aḥmad b. Hanbal then know that this man is a man of the Sunnah."

Imām Qutaybah said in *Ḥilyat al-Awliyā'*, vol.9, p.168 that, "Had there been no Aḥmad b. Hanbal then religious zeal would have died."

His Teachers

Some of his famous teachers were: Imām ash-Shafi'i, Imām Sufyān b. Uyayna, and many more.

His Students

Some of his famous students were: Imām Bukhārī, Imām Muslim, Imām Abū Dāwūd and many more.

Books

Some of his famous books are: *Musnad*, which is a compilation of around 30,000 Aḥādīth; *Virtues of the Companions*, and many more.

Death

He died in the year 241 Hijrī at the age of around 77 years old, corresponding to 857 AD.

It is reported by Imām adh-Dhahabi that there were as many as 800,000 men and 60,000 women at his funeral.

'Alī b. Ḥajar b. Ayyās as-Sa'dī al-Marwazī al-Baghdādī (d. 244 Hijrī) described his sorrow by reading the following poem at the death of Imām Aḥmad b. Hanbal. As mentioned in *al-Jarh Wa Ta'dil*, vol.1, p.313:

Ibrahim informed me of the most pious person in the world;

More than whom the name of a well-respected person did not reach our ears;

He was an Imām who walked on the straight path and the Sunnah of the Prophet (ﷺ);

[on the path of] The honest and last Messenger of Allāh;

He bore with patience whatever difficulty came upon him and had reliance;

Upon his Rabb, in a manner where he fulfilled the right of reliance upon his Rabb;

So I said, and tears overflowed on my chest from all four sides;

Like the broken layers of pearls;

May salam equal to the amount of sand, stars and drops of rain;

Be upon Aḥmad, the righteous and pious, son of Ḥanbal;

Wake up and prepare for death;

Since life is indeed short o 'Alī [b. Ḥajar];

As if you are sleeping taking the palm as a pillow;

And soon you are forgotten after being taken to a frightening place;

You will stay here and the sand [around] your grave;

Will be flown around due to the fast winds from the North and South.

The information for the biography has been taken from many different accounts. For more details on the life of Imām Aḥmad consult the various books available in various languages. The most popular ones being *Manaqib al-Imām Aḥmad* by Ibn al-Jawzī and biographical accounts such as *Siyar 'Alam an-Nubalā* and *Tarīkh ul-Islām* by Imām adh-Dhahabī.

مواعظ الإمام أحمد بن حنبل

ADVICE and ADMONITIONS

Imām Aḥmad b. Ḥanbal

[1] As-Sunnah

Imām Aḥmad said:

> The foundations of the Sunnah according to us (are):
>
> Clinging on to what the companions of the Messenger of Allāh ﷺ were upon and emulating them; forsaking innovation as every innovation is misguidance; forsaking arguments, debates and controversies about the religion.
>
> So the Sunnah according to us are the narrations of the Messenger of Allāh ﷺ. The Sunnah is the interpretation of the Quran and its demonstrative evidences. There is neither *Qiyās* (analogy) in the Sunnah nor are examples drawn from it, and it is not comprehended by intellects or whims; it is only compliance and forsaking desire.[1]

[2] The Companion of Ḥadīth

Abūl Qāsim b. Manīʿ[2] said: I wanted to leave (home) to (visit) Suwaid b. Saʿīd[3], so I asked Aḥmad b. Ḥanbal to write to him [Suwaid]. So [Aḥmad] wrote: "And this man writes Ḥadīth." So I said: "O Abū 'Abdillāh! (What

---

1. Ibn al-Jawzī, *Manāqib al-Imām Aḥmad*, p. 171.

2. [EN] Abūl Qāsim b. Manīʿ was a student of Imām Aḥmad b. Hanbal who compiled unique issues from him. *Tarīkh Baghdad,* vol. 11, p. 325.

3. [EN] Suwaid b. Saʿīd was a narrator of ḥadīth. *Tarīkh Baghdad,* vol. 9, p.227.

about) my service to you and attachment? If only you had written: This man is among the Companions of Ḥadīth (*Aṣḥāb al-Ḥadīth*)." So [Aḥmad] replied: "The Companion of Ḥadīth according to us is one who implements Ḥadīth."[4]

[3] Truth And Falsehood

It was said to Imām Aḥmad during the days of the *Miḥnah* (trial)[5]: "O Abū ʿAbdillāh! Have you not seen the truth; how it prevails over falsehood?" To which Aḥmad replied: "Never! Indeed the prevalence of falsehood over truth is when the hearts turn from guidance towards misguidance. But our hearts remain firm to the truth."[6]

[4] Ignorance Does Not Harm

Al-Marwazī[7] said: Imām Aḥmad was asked once about *Yaʾjūj* and *Maʾjūj*[8]:

---

4. Ibn al-Jawzī, *Manāqib al-Imām Aḥmad*, p. 208. The meaning of this is that [Aḥmad] would not say (about Abūl Qāsim): "A Companion of Ḥadīth" unless he would implement and act upon Ḥadīth. Thereby, recording Ḥadīth did not grant [Abūl Qāsim] this description. This is from Imām Aḥmad's precision in defining the meaning of technical terms, and the truthfulness when clarifying the level of men and their ranks. So the man's service to Imām Aḥmad did not intercede on his behalf whereby he could earn a title that he is not worthy of.

5. [EN] The term *Miḥnah* is generally used to refer to a trial or ordeal. Historically when it is mentioned alongside Imām Aḥmad then this is in reference to the religious test and persecution inaugurated by al-Maʾmun. The issue at hand was regarding the creation of the Qurʾan due to the Muʿtazilities doctrine. Generally the Miḥnah extended from the year 218 to 234 *Hijrī*. Ali b. Al-Madīnī said, "Allāh fortified this religion through two men, and there is not a third with them: Abu Bakr As-Siddīq 🙵 on the Day of Apostasy, and Ahmad b. Hanbal on the day of the *Miḥnah* (trial)." *Tabaqāt al-Hanābilah*, 1/227.

6. Ibn al-Jawzī, *Manāqib al-Imām Aḥmad*, p. 311.

7. [EN] He is Abū Bakr al-Marwazī and was one of the most formidable contemporaries of Imām Aḥmad b. Ḥanbal. Abū Bakr b. Sadaqah said: "I have not known anyone who defended the religion of Allāh more than al-Marwazī." *Siyar Aʾlam an-Nubalā*, vol. 10, p. 315.

8. [EN] Gog and Magog.

"Are they Muslim?" So [Aḥmad] said to the questioner: "Have I mastered knowledge whereby you could ask such a thing?"[9]

[5] The Most Virtuous Actions

Muhannā[10] said: I asked Aḥmad: "Narrate to us what are the most virtuous actions?" [Aḥmad] replied: "Seeking knowledge." I asked: "For whom?" [Aḥmad] replied: "For whoever corrects his intention." I asked: "And what thing corrects his intention?" [Aḥmad] replied: "He intends that he is humbled during it, and ignorance is expelled from him."[11]

[6] Clear Disbelief

Abū Ṭālib[12] said: It was related from al-Karābīsī[13] that he mentioned [Allāh] the Most High's statement,

﴿ الْيَوْمَ أَكْمَلْتُ لَكُمْ دِينَكُمْ ﴾

"Today I have perfected for you all your religion," [Quran, 5:3]

And said: "Had our religion been perfected for us, there would not have been these differences of opinion!" So Imām Aḥmad replied: "This is clear disbelief (*kufr*)!"[14]

---

9. *Al-Ādāb ash-Shar'iyyah*, vol. 2, p. 72.

10. [EN] His full name is Muhannā b. Yaḥyā Abū Abdillāh from the senior students of Imām Aḥmad b. Ḥanbal. *Tarīkh Baghdad,* vol. 13, p. 266.

11. *Al-Ādāb ash-Shar'iyyah*, vol. 2, p. 38.

12. [EN] His full name is Aḥmad b. Humaid, Abū Ṭālib al-Mishkani from the senior students of Imām Aḥmad b. Hanbal who reported unique issues from him. *Tarīkh Baghdād,* vol. 4, p.344.

13. [EN] Al-Karābīsī was declared as a *Jahmi* and innovator by Imām Aḥmad b. Hanbal. *At-Ṭabaqāt,* vol. 1, p. 41, and *Tarīkh Baghdād,* vol. 8, p. 65.

14. *Al-Maqṣid al-Arshad,* vol. 1, p. 96.

[7] Ennobling Oneself

Imām Aḥmad purchased some flour and he commissioned Ayūb al-Ḥammāl[15]; then [Ayūb] carried it with [Aḥmad] to the latter's house and [Ahmad] found inside (the house) some bread and Ayub saw it. So Aḥmad said to his son Ṣāliḥ: "Give [Ayūb] two loaves of bread." But [Ayūb] refused them and left. Then Aḥmad said to his son: "Catch up with him with these [loaves]." So [Ṣāliḥ] did so and [Ayūb] took the two [loaves] and Ṣāliḥ was astonished (by this). So Aḥmad said: "Do not be surprised! His ego considered himself deserving of the bread when he saw it, so he refused it. But when he left he relinquished hope (for the bread). So when I gifted it to him he accepted it."[16]

[8] Dark Piety

Imām Aḥmad would take out his inkpot to draw (ink) from it and a man sought his permission to write from his inkpot. So [Aḥmad] said to him: "Write, for this is dark piety (*Wara' Muẓlim*)!"[17] Then another man sought permission for the same thing so [Aḥmad] smiled and said: "Neither my piety or your piety reaches here or there (this or that inkpot!)"[18]

---

15. [TN] Ayūb al-Ḥammāl (*lit.* the load-carrier or porter) was a contemporary of Imām Aḥmad who lived in Baghdad. He was widely known for his asceticism and piety. *Tārīkh Baghdād,* vol. 7, p. 8.

16. *At-Taysīr bi Sharḥ al-Jawāmiʿ as-Ṣaghīr*, vol. 1, p. 353. It is related in a ḥadīth agreed upon (by al-Bukhārī [no. 1473] and Muslim [no. 1045]): "If there comes to you anything from this wealth and you are neither a greedy person (*mushraf*) nor a beggar, then take it, but if not then do not allow yourself to chase it." There is no surprise in this matter about the *Fiqh* of Imām Aḥmad, but the surprise is from the *Fiqh* of Ayūb al-Ḥammāl.

17. [TN] *Waraʿ*, translated here as piety, is to leave any matter which would harm a person in the hereafter; as such, it is *Waraʿ* to leave the unlawful matters; some of the *Salaf* would leave doubtful matters out of *Waraʿ*. According to Shaykh Turkmānī, Imām Aḥmad referred to piety here as dark in a play on words, referencing the black ink to signify that the man's request was misplaced, and not an act of piety; in other words, he need not ask permission for such a minor and lawful thing.

18. *Jāmiʿ al-ʿUlūm wa 'l-Ḥikam*, vol. 1, p. 111.

[9] Fair-mindedness

Imām Aḥmad said:

> It is required for the fair-minded person to possess six qualities:
>
> - (He should have) jurisprudential knowledge (*Faqīh*);
> - Be a scholar in general (*ʿĀlim*);
> - Be an ascetic (*Zāhid*);
> - Be pious (*Waraʿ*);
> - Be chaste (*ʿAfīf*);
> - Foreseeing (*Baṣīr*) of what it is (likely) to occur; discerning (*Baṣīr*) of what has transpired.[19]

[10] Taking the Means

Abūl -Q̰āsim b. al-Khatalī[20] said: I asked Aḥmad b. Ḥanbal: "What do you say about a man who sits in his home or the Masjid and says: "I won't work at all until my sustenance comes to me." To which Aḥmad said:

> This man is bereft of knowledge. Have you not heard the statement of the Messenger of Allāh ﷺ: "[Allāh] made my provision under the shade of my spear"[21], the other ḥadīth which mentions a bird that goes out in the morning[22] -Then he mentioned that the bird goes out in search of provision- and [Allāh's] statement, the Most High:
>
> ﴿ وَآخَرُونَ يَضْرِبُونَ فِي الْأَرْضِ يَبْتَغُونَ مِن فَضْلِ اللَّهِ ﴾
>
> "And others will travel the earth yearning of Allāh's bounty..." [Q̰uran, 73:20]?"[23]

---

19. *Al-Maqṣid al-Arshad*, vol. 3, p. 164.

20. [EN] His full name is Abul Q̰asim, Ishāq b. Ibrahim b. Sinin al-Khatalī. He was attributed to Khatlan which is near Samarqand. He was a narrator of Ḥadīth. *Tarīkh Baghdad*, vol. 6, p. 381.

21. [TN] Reported by Aḥmad in *al-Musnad* (4869).

22. [TN] Reported by at-Tirmidhī in *al-Jāmiʿ* (2344).

23. *Talblīs Iblīs*, vol. 1, p. 347.

[11] Al-Layth b. Saʿd[24] [d. 175 A.H.]

Imām Aḥmad said:

> Al-Layth is full of knowledge; sound in ḥadīth. Among the Egyptians none is more precise than him; how sound is his Ḥadīth! I saw who I saw but I have never seen anyone like him! He was a complete scholar of Jurisprudence (*Faqīh al-Badan*); eloquent in Arabic; proficient in the Quran and in [Arabic] grammar; he memorised Ḥadīth and poetry; proficient in revision...

And [Aḥmad] enumerated (other) beautiful characteristics about [al-Layth].[25]

[12] The Remembrance of Death

Imām Aḥmad said:

> When I remember death, everything in the matters of this *Dunyā* becomes easy [for me]. And [this *Dunyā*] is but food and then no food; clothing and then no clothing. Indeed these are a short number of days and I am not straightened by poverty at all.

Al-Marwazī said: When Imām Aḥmad would remember death, his weeping [and grief] would choke him, and he would say: "Fear prevents me from consuming food and drink."[26]

---

24. [EN] He was from the senior students of the *Tābi'ūn*. He was ranked as an Imām and leading authority of Islamic knowledge and jurisprudence in the early years of Islām. *Siyar A'lam an-Nubalā,* vol. 8, p. 137

25. *Tahdhīb al-Asmā'*, vol. 2, p. 382.

26. Adh-Dhahabī, *Tārīkh al-Islām,* vol. 18, p. 81.

[13] Knowledge Takes Precedence Over Supererogatory Acts

ʿAbdullāh, the son of Imām Aḥmad, said: When Abū Zurʿah[27] arrived, he stayed with my father and he would engage in many discussions with him. So I heard my father saying one day: "I have not prayed (anything) besides the obligatory (prayers). I chose discourse with Abū Zurʿah over my supererogatory acts."[28]

[14] The Honour of Hearts

Imām Aḥmad said: "Indeed everything has an honour, and the honour of the heart is being in a state of contentment with Allāh."[29]

[15] Seeking Coarseness

ʿAbdullāh said: I sat by my father ﷺ one day, and he looked at my two feet and they were both smooth bearing no cracks. So he said to me: "What's with these feet? Why don't you walk barefoot until your legs become coarse?"[30]

---

27. [EN] His name is Ubaidillah b. 'Abd al-Karīm ar-Rāzī. He was one of the scholars of Ḥadīth during the time of Imām Aḥmad. He was from Rey, in modern day Iran, and an Imām in Ḥadīth. Many people have praised his level of memorisation. Adh-Dhahabī describes him as one of the Imams and *Ḥāfiẓ* of the era. *Tadhkirat al-Ḥuffāẓ*, vol. 2, p. 136

28. *Al-Ādāb ash-Sharʿiyyah*, vol. 2, p. 165.

29. *Manāqib al-Imām Aḥmad*, p. 201.

30. *Tārīkh Madīnat Damishq*, vol. 5, p. 298.

[EN] The Prophet ﷺ used to command his companions to walk barefoot sometimes, *Sunan Abī Dāwūd* no.4160; graded *Saḥīḥ* by Shaikh al-Albānī. Mulla 'Alī Qārī explained that "The wisdom behind this is to accustom the soul to coarseness, to distance it from ease, to normalize it to asceticism, and to despise the world." *Mirqāt al-Mafātiḥ*, vol. 7, pg. 2827.

Shaikh Ibn ʿUthaymīn explained that, "Wearing shoes is from the Sunnah and walking barefoot sometimes is also from the Sunnah. The reason being because the Prophet ﷺ forbade excessive luxury, and therefore commanded walking barefoot sometimes." *Sharh Riyadh us-Salihin*, vol. 6, p. 387.

[16] The *Dunyā* and the Sultan

Imām Aḥmad said: "The *Dunyā* is a disease; the Sultan a remedy; the scholar a doctor. But if you see the doctor dragging the disease towards himself, then be wary of him!"[31]

[17] Asceticism

Imām Aḥmad said: "Asceticism (*Zuhd*) in the *Dunyā* is: restricted aspiration and despair of what people possess."[32]

[18] Maʿrūf al-Karkhī

During one of Aḥmad's gatherings, the condition of Maʿrūf al-Karkhī[33] was mentioned; some of those present said, "He has little knowledge." Then Aḥmad said: "Refrain! May Allāh pardon you! Does he choose of knowledge except what reaches him which is good (*Maʿrūf*)?"[34]

= Shaikh ʿAbdul-Muḥsin al-ʿAbbād explained that, "If there are things on the ground that necessitate wearing shoes, then a person should wear shoes. If the ground, for example, has glass or iron, or there are stones or thorns on it, or sand in the intense heat of the sun. So a person should make use of this protection that Allāh has bestowed and blessed upon him, which is the use of slippers (or shoes)." *Sharḥ Sunan Abī Dāwūd*, 23/273.

31. *Tārīkh Madinat Dimishq*, vol. 5, p. 298.

32. *Ṭabaqāt al-Ḥanābilah*, vol. 1, p. 39.

33. [TN] Maʿrūf al-Karkhī was a renowned ascetic; he was buried in Baghdad in the year 200 *Hijri*. Adh-Dhahabī, *Siyar Aʿlām an-Nubalā,* vol. 9, p. 340. [EN] When he was questioned "What are the signs of the *Awliyā*?" He said: "There are three things: their concerns are for Allāh, their preoccupation with Him, and their flight to Him." *Ḥilyatul Awlīyā,* vol. 8, p. 412.

34. *Mukhtaṣar al-Muʿammal*, vol. 1, p. 74.

[19] *At-Taghāful*[35]

In response to a man who said, "Wellness (*Āfiyah*)[36] consists of ten parts, nine of which involve *at-Taghāful*", Imām Aḥmad replied, "Wellness (*Āfiyah*) consists of ten parts: all of them involve *at-Taghāful*."[37]

[20] The Taste of Relief

Muḥammad b. Ḥasnawaih said: "I was in the presence of Abū ʿAbdillāh Aḥmad b. Ḥanbal, and a man questioned him and said: "When will the slave (of Allāh) find the taste of relief?" So [Aḥmad] said to him: "When he takes his first step into Paradise."[38]

[21] The Slaves (of Allāh) on the Day of Judgement

Imām Aḥmad said:

> Indeed Allāh will resurrect the slaves (of Allāh) on the Day of Judgement with one of three traits:
>
> [1] The good-doer upon whom there is no blame, due to [Allāh's] saying, the Most High:
>
> ﴿ مَا عَلَى الْمُحْسِنِينَ مِن سَبِيلٍ ﴾
>
> "There is no blame on the good-doers." [Quran, 9:91]
>
> [2] The disbeliever in the Fire, due to [Allāh's] saying, the Most High:
>
> ﴿ وَالَّذِينَ كَفَرُوا لَهُمْ نَارُ جَهَنَّمَ ﴾

35. [TN] *At-taghāful* refers to the act of overlooking a matter, and pretending to be unmindful of it. For example, a man intentionally overlooks something he dislikes about his wife, and vice versa.

36. [TN] The full meaning of *Āfiyah* is being in a state of good health, free from illness and grief, away from all problems, pains, harms and sufferings. This can be achieved through *Taghāful*.

37. *Al-Furūʿ*, vol. 5, p. 261.

38. *Al-Maqṣid al-Arshad*, vol. 2, p. 398.

"And those who disbelieve, for them is the Fire of Jahannam..." [Quran, 35: 36]

[3] Those who sinned and erred, and their affair is with Allāh; if He wills, He will punish (them), and if He wills, He will forgive them, due to [Allāh's] saying, the Most High:

﴿ إِنَّ اللَّهَ لَا يَغْفِرُ أَن يُشْرَكَ بِهِ وَيَغْفِرُ مَا دُونَ ذَٰلِكَ لِمَن يَشَاءُ ۚ وَمَن يُشْرِكْ بِاللَّهِ فَقَدِ افْتَرَىٰ إِثْمًا عَظِيمًا ﴾

"Indeed Allāh does not forgive that anything is associated with Him but He forgives anything less than that to whomsoever He wills." [Quran, 4:48 and 116][39]

[22] Take Knowledge Face-to-Face

Qutaibah b. Sa'īd[40] said: I arrived in Baghdad and I had no other intention other than to meet Aḥmad b. Ḥanbal. It was then that he came to me accompanied with Yaḥyā b. Ma'īn and they both discussed (knowledge) with me. Then Aḥmad b. Ḥanbal stood up and sat before me and said: "Dictate this to me." Then we revised. Then [Yaḥyā] also stood up and sat before me so I said: "O Aba 'Abdillāh! Sit in your (original) place." So he replied: "Do not concern yourself with me. Indeed I only wish to take knowledge (in the correct and best manner) face-to-face!"[41]

[23] Precision in the Prophetic *Ḥadīth*

Imām Aḥmad said: "We would write down Ḥadīth from six places or seven places, (still) we did not consider it precise. Then how will the one who records [a Ḥadīth] from a single place be sure he is precise?"[42]

---

39. Ibid, vol. 1, p. 188.

40. [EN] Qutaibah b. Sa'īd was an Imām and scholar of Ḥadīth. He was born in Balkh which is in modern day Afghanistan. A significant amount of Aḥādīth are reported from him by the famous scholars of the six books of Ḥadīth. He had many famous teachers and students. Adh-Dhahabī declared him as Shaikh ul-Islām. *Siyar 'Alam an-Nubalā*, vol. 11, p. 14

41. Ibn al-Jawzī, *Manāqib al-Imām Aḥmad*, p. 57.

42. Ibid, p. 58.

[24] A Morsel (of Food) in His Brother's Mouth

Ismā'īl b. al-Alā[43] said: Al-Kalwadhānī, Rizq Allāh b. Mūsā[44], called me and he brought over to us a large amount of food. Among the people (there in the gathering) was Aḥmad b. Ḥanbal, Yaḥyā b. Ma'īn, Abū Khaithamah and others. So [Al-Kalwadhānī] brought out *lūzīnj*[45] for which he had spent 80 dirhams on. Then Abū Khaithamah said: "This is extravagance!" And Aḥmad said: "No! If the *Dunyā* was to be gathered into a single morsel of food, and then a Muslim man was to take it and put it in the mouth of his Muslim brother, he would not have been extravagant!" And Yaḥyā said: "You are right, O Abū 'Abdillāh!"[46]

[25] Goodness

Imām Aḥmad said: "Goodness is in the one who sees no good in himself!"[47]

[26] The Successful Person

Imām Aḥmad said: "O my son! The successful one is whoever succeeds tomorrow (i.e. in the hereafter) and there is no one he leaves behind with a claim (against him)."[48]

---

43. [EN] His statements are mentioned in books such as *Manāqib al-Imām Aḥmad* and *al-Maqṣid al-Arshad.*

44. [EN] Rizq Allāh b. Mūsā, Abū Bakr an-Naji. It is also said that he is named Abū 'l-Faḍl al-Baghdādī al-Iskafi al-Kalwadhānī. He was a trustworthy narrator of Ḥadīth and reported from a group of major scholars such as Yaḥyā b. Sa'īd al-Qaṭṭān, Sufyān b. Uyaynah and other than them. The likes of an-Nasā'ī and Ibn Mājah narrate from him. *Tarīkh al-Islām* vol. 6, p. 81.

45. [EN] A type of Persian semi-flaky dessert that is a pastry served with almond spread.

46. *Ṭabaqāt al-Ḥanābilah*, vol. 1, p. 106.

47. *Dhayl Ṭabaqāt al-Ḥanābilah*, vol. 1, p. 305.

48. *Tārīkh Madinat Dimishq*, vol. 5, p. 308.

[27] The Supererogatory *Ḥajj*

Imām Aḥmad was asked about a man, should he perform a supererogatory *Ḥajj* or spend (its cost) on his relatives in need? And he replied: "That he places it into starving stomachs is more beloved to me."[49]

[28] The Importance of the *Rabbāniyūn*[50] Scholars

Imām Aḥmad said:

> All praise belongs to Allāh who made in every era those who remain among the people of knowledge: they call the astray to guidance, and they forbid (that which leads to) ruin; they revive the dead (hearts), the ignoramuses and the damned, by the Book of Allāh, and by the Sunnah of the Prophet (ﷺ). How many murdered victims of Iblīs have they revived and how many among the wandering astray have they guided! How excellent is their impact on the people! They defend the religion of Allāh against the distortions of the extremists, and the pretences of the nullifiers: those who believe in foolish innovations, and let loose the reigns of discord, who contradict the Book, attributing things to Allāh, or saying things about Him – high above is Allāh from what the oppressors say, High and Mighty – or about His Book without knowledge.[51]

49. *Al-Furūʿ*, vol. 2, p. 497.

50. [TN] The *Rabbānī* scholar is defined in various ways including one who possesses great knowledge, who combines between much knowledge and acts of worship, who nurtures students with minor matters of knowledge before introducing them to major ones, etc.

51. Ibn al-Jawzī, *Manāqib al-Imām Aḥmad*, p. 167.

[29] The Bearers (*Ḥamalat*) of the Qur'ān[52]

Imām Aḥmad said: "It is beloved to me that the hearts of men whose chests retain the Qur'an melt away the *Dunyā.*"[53]

[30] The Path of Acquiring Knowledge

Khalaf[54] said: Aḥmad b. Ḥanbal came to me in order to hear the ḥadīth of Abū 'Awānah and I tried to lift him up to seat him in an elevated position (above myself) but he refused and said: "I will not sit except facing you. We were ordered to behave humbly towards those we learn from!"[55]

[31] The Ascetic Possesses a Thousand Dinars

Imām Aḥmad was asked about a man who possesses a thousand dinars, can he be an ascetic (*Zāhid*)? He replied: "Yes, with the condition that he is not delighted if he gained more or saddened if it decreases."[56]

---

52. [TN] The *Hamalat* (bearers) of the Qur'an are those who act upon it even if they do not memorise it all. See al-Ājurrī, *Ādāb Ḥamalat al-Qur'ān.*

53. Ibn al-Jawzī, *Manāqib al-Imām Aḥmad,* p. 200. The meaning here is that it is not befitting for a scholar who becomes cognizant of the Noble Qur'an, nor a *Ḥāfiẓ* who has memorised the Book of Allāh, the Most High, to be deeply occupied and devoted by the *Dunyā,* running out of breadth after it, and severely disappointed by its passing if he does not catch up to it.

54. [EN] He is Khalaf b. Hisham b. Tha'lab. It is also said his name is Khalaf b. Hisham b. Ṭālib b. Ghurab. He was a person of the *Sunnah* and was a worshipper. *Tarīkh Baghdad* vol. 9, p. 270

55. Ibn al-Jawzī, *Manāqib al-Imām Aḥmad,* p. 58.

56. *Fayḍ al-Qadīr,* vol. 4, p. 73.

[32] The Shining Bright Light of Islam

Al-Faḍl b. Aḥmad az-Zubaidī[57] said: I heard Aḥmad b. Ḥanbal, when the *Aṣḥāb al-Ḥadīth* came to (him) with inkpots in their hands, and he signalled to one of them and said: "These (*Aṣḥāb al-Ḥadīth*) are the shining bright light of Islam."[58]

[33] Supplication[59]

'Abdullāh b. Imām Aḥmad said: I heard my father saying while in prostration: "O Allāh! Just as You protected my face from prostrating to other than You, then guard my face from asking other than You!"[60]

57. [EN] He is Al-Faḍl b. Aḥmad b. Mansur b. ath-Thayal, Abul Abbas az-Zubaidī. He was a trustworthy narrator. *Tarīkh Baghdād* vol. 14, p. 353

58. *Al-Ādab ash-Shar'iyyah*, vol. 2, p. 58.

59. [EN] Supplication is to ask Allāh. Supplication is worship. *Saḥīḥ at-Tirmidhī* no.2590. Ibn Battal said: "The believer should strive hard in offering supplication, and he should have hope of receiving a response. He should not despair of the mercy of Allāh, because he is calling upon One Who is most generous. This was referred to in *mutawātir* reports from the Prophet ﷺ." *Sharh Saḥīḥ al-Bukhārī,* vol. 10, p. 90.

Ibn Hajar said: "Every supplicant receives a response, but the response varies. Sometimes he gets exactly what he prayed for, and sometimes he gets something else as compensation. This is mentioned in a Saḥīḥ hadith." *Fatḥ al-Bārī,* vol. 11, p. 95.

Shaykh Ibn Bāz said: "So the individual should persist in offering supplication and think positively of Allāh, may He be glorified and exalted, and he should know that He is all-wise, all-knowing; He may hasten the response for a reason, or He may delay it for a reason, or He may give the supplicant something better than what he asked for." *Majmū' Fatāwā Ibn Bāz,* vol. 9, p 353.

Ibn Rajab said: "Sa'īd b. Manṣūr narrated, with his chain, that Abū Salamah said: Some of the companions of the Messenger of Allah ﷺ came together and discussed the hour (of response) on Friday, and when they parted they all agreed that it is the last hour of Friday." *Fatḥ al-Bārī*, vol. 8, p. 302-303.

60. *Maṭālib Ūlīn -Nāhī*, vol. 1, p. 463.

[34] The Etiquette of Writing

Aḥmad b. Ḥanbal preferred that when a young person would write to a senior that the former put the recipient's name first; as for him [Aḥmad], he would begin with the recipient's name, whether he was senior or junior, out of humility.[61]

[35] Consistent in What He Loves

Imām Aḥmad said: "If you would like Allāh to grant you continuity in what you love, then be consistent in what He loves."[62]

[36] Human Dignity

Imām Aḥmad was asked about a man who makes a vow to make *Ṭawāf* around the House (al-Kaʿbah) on all fours? To which he replied: "He makes *Ṭawāf* two times and he should not make *Ṭawāf* on all fours."[63]

[37] Sins Decrease *Īmān*

Imām Aḥmad said: *Īmān* is statements and deeds. It increases and decreases,

61. *Fatḥ al-Mughīth,* vol. 2, p. 136.

62. *Al-Ādab ash-Sharʿiyyah*, vol. 2, p. 31.

63. *Manāqib al-Imām Aḥmad,* p. 65. Ibn al-Jawzī commented on this as follows: "So look at this understanding: it was as though [Imām Aḥmad] considered the (man's) falling down on his face, and saw this as a precedent (which others would follow) and a departure from the form of a human into that of resembling a beast. So he protected the man, and he protected the House and Masjid from this (act); but he did not cancel the ruling from his wording of walking on the two hands, but the man would have to do so with his two legs which are the tools for walking." I say: Thus, the Imām did not forsake the general principles and objectives of the Shar'iah while he issued fatwas on a subsidiary issue.

and all of righteousness is part of *Īmān*, and sins decrease *Īmān*.[64]

[38] Honouring the Companions

Imām Aḥmad said: "If you see a man mentioning anyone of the Companions of the Messenger of Allah ﷺ badly, then suspect his Islām.[65]

[39] Islām and the Sunnah

Al-Ḥasan b. Ayyūb al-Baghdādī[66] said: It was said to Abū 'Abdullāh Aḥmad b. Ḥanbal: "May Allah resurrect you upon Islām!" So he replied: "...and the Sunnah"[67]

[40] The Expiation for Breaking an Oath

'Abdullāh b. Imām Aḥmad said: When death approached upon Imām Aḥmad, he removed a purse from his pocket in which there contained the amount of two silver dirhams. Then he said: "Expiate on my behalf the expiation of breaking one oath; indeed I think that I broke an oath once during my life ."[68]

---

64. *Manāqib al-Imām Aḥmad*, p. 153.

65. *Manāqib al-Imām Aḥmad*, p. 160.

66. [TN] He narrated some statements from Imām Aḥmad in *Manāqib al-Imām Aḥmad* and *Al-Maqṣid al-Arshad*. *Tarīkh Baghdad* vol. 8, p. 235.

67. *Ibid*, p. 177. The statement of the Imām "And the Sunnah" is from his (great) comprehension, may Allāh have mercy on him. For there is found among some of the Muslim sects those who curse the Companions ﷺ, while in the *Ṣaḥīḥ* [the Prophet ﷺ] said: "Do not curse my Companions! Indeed if one of you were to spend the like of (Mount) Uhud in gold, you would not amount to the Mudd (approx. 750g) of one of them nor half of that." So whoever does so then he is a Muslim but he is not following the Sunnah, and his Islām is doubted. Had it not been for the generation of the Companions and their Jihad, then indeed Islām would not have reached us!

68. *Tārīkh Madīnat Damishq*, vol. 5, p. 325.

[41] The Zakāt of Knowledge

ʿAbdullāh b. Jaʿfar[69] said: I heard Aḥmad b. Ḥanbal say when he was asked about a man who records Ḥadīth then increases them (to record more): "It is required to act by it , according to the amount that he increases in seeking (knowledge by recording it)."[70] Then he said: "The path of knowledge is like the path of wealth: when wealth increases, one's Zakāt increases."[71]

[42] Sit With the People

Hārūn b. ʿAbdullāh al-Ḥammāl[72] said: Aḥmad b. Ḥanbal came to me during the night and he knocked on my door. So I said: "Who is this?" and he replied: "It is me, Aḥmad." So I hurried to him and he embraced me and I embraced him. I said: "Do you need something O Aba ʿAbdillāh?" And he replied: "Yes. You occupied my heart today." I said: "How so, O Abū ʿAbdillāh?" He replied: "I passed by you while you were sitting in the shade narrating to the people and they were under the Sun. In their hands were pens and notebooks. Do not do that again. When you sit, sit with the people!"[73]

[43] Heedlessness

Al-ʿAbbās b. Ḥamzah[74] said: I heard Aḥmad b. Ḥanbal say: "Perfect You

---

69. [EN] His statements are mentioned in books such as *Manāqib al-Imām Aḥmad* and *al-Maqṣid al-Arshad.*

70. [EN] Meaning the more knowledge you seek and obtain the more you will have to put into practice.

71. *Al-Ādāb ash-Sharʿiyyah*, vol. 2, no. 167.

72. [EN] He was an Imām and heard ḥadīth from notable scholars such as Sufyān b. Uyaynah. He was called *al-Ḥammāl* (the load bearer or porter) because he carried a man on the road to Makkah on his back. *Siyar A'lam an-Nubalā* vol. 12, p. 115

73. Ibn al-Jawzī, *Manāqib al-Imām Aḥmad,* p. 220.

74. [EN] Al-ʿAbbās b. Ḥamzah b. ʾAbdullāh. He was a preacher and eloquent. *Tārīkh Damishq* Vol. 26, p. 245

are (O Allāh, *Subḥānak*)! How heedless are the creation about what lays before them. The fearful one among them is negligent while the hopeful one among them is weak!"[75]

[44] Who Talks About *al-Wara'*?

Imām Aḥmad was asked a matter pertaining to *al-Wara'*, so he said: "It is not fitting for me to talk about this when I eat from the produce of Baghdad. Had Bishr been here it would have been befitting for him to speak."[76]

[45] The Need For Knowledge

Imām Aḥmad said:

> People are more in need of knowledge than they are of food and drink because a man needs food and drink once or twice a day. (Whilst) his need for knowledge is (equivalent to) the number of his breaths (that he takes).

He further said: We narrated from Ash-Shafi'i (May Allāh be pleased with him) that he said: "Seeking knowledge is better than (performing) supererogatory prayers."[77]

---

75. *Tārīkh Madīnat Damishq*, vol. 5, p. 324.

76. *Al-Istikhrāj li-Aḥkām al-Khirāj*, vol. 1, p. 111. Bishr b. al-Ḥārith (al-Ḥāfī) would not eat from the produce of Baghdad and he would censure those that did.
Imām Aḥmad said:
"The only thing that empowered Bishr to do so was because he was alone and had no family. The reason for this was that 'Umar ﷺ endowed the rural areas of Iraq to the Muslims. But during a case of necessity, it is permitted for a man to eat from its lands and to feed his family."

77. *Madarij as-Salikin* vol. 2, p.470

[46] *At-Tawakkul*

Imām Aḥmad was asked about *at-Tawakkul*[78] so he replied: "It is to cut off raising one's expectations by despairing of the creation." It was said to him: "And what is the proof for this?" He replied: The statement of Ibrāhīm 🙶 when he was placed in the catapult and hurled into the fire (pit). Jibrīl 🙶 intercepted him and said: 'Is there a need (for my help)?' He replied: 'With respect from you, then no.' So [Jibrīl] said: 'Then ask whom you have a need of.' So [Ibrāhīm] said: 'The more beloved of the two things to me is whatsoever is more beloved to Him (Allāh).'"[79]

[47] The Levels of Asceticism

Imām Aḥmad said:

Asceticism (*Az-Zuhd*) is of three kinds:

[1] Leaving the forbidden (things), and this is the asceticism of the common people.

[2] Leaving the unnecessary (and extravagant) things from the lawful matters, and this is the asceticism of the adept (*al-Khawwāṣ*).

[3] Leaving whatsoever busies (and distracts) oneself from Allāh, and this is the asceticism of the cognisant (*al-ʿĀrifīn*).[80]

[48] The Completeness of a Meal

Imām Aḥmad said: "When a meal combines four things then it is complete:

---

78. [TN] *At-Tawakkul* is to rely on Allāh alone without forfeiting the means.

79. *Tārīkh Madīnat Damishq*, vol. 5, p. 308.

80. *Madārij al-Sālikīn*, vol. 2, no. 12. Imām Ibn Qayyim commented on this as follows: "And this statement of Imām Aḥmad follows on from all what has preceded from the words of (other scholars), but it offers more detail and clarifies its levels. It is the most comprehensive explanation (of it). It demonstrates that [Imām Aḥmad] had the greatest knowledge of this quality. Ash-Shāfiʿī attested to [Imām Aḥmad's] pre-eminence in eight matters, one of which was asceticism."

When one remembers Allāh in the beginning; praises Him at the end; when many hands share in it; it is from the lawful."[81]

[49] Intention

Al-Faḍl b. Ziyād[82] said: I asked Aba 'Abdillāh (Imām Aḥmad) about intention during action. I said: "How is this intention made?" He replied: "One should attend to his self: when he intends an action, he should not desire (the acknowledgement) of people by doing it." Yazīd b. Hārūn narrated the ḥadīth of 'Umar ﷺ: "Actions are by intentions" and Aḥmad was present. Aḥmad said to Yazīd: "O Abū Khālid! This is *Khunāq* (strangulation i.e. a truly difficult and suffocating matter)!"[83]

[50] In What Condition Did You Awaken?

Abū Bakr al-Marwazī said: I visited Aḥmad one day and said to him: "In what condition did you awaken?" So he replied:

> How should one awaken whose *Rabb* seeks of him the fulfilment of obligations; His Prophet seeks of him the fulfilment of the Sunnah; the two Angels seek of him correct deeds; his self seeks of him its desires; Iblīs seeks of him indecent sins; the Angel of Death seeks of him the taking of his soul; and his family seeks of him spending?[84]

81. As-Suyūṭī, *Ash-Shamā'il ash-Sharīfah,* vol. 1, no. 316.

82. [EN] He is Al-Faḍl b. Ziyād, Abul 'Abbās al-Qattan al-Baghdadi. He reported many issues pertaining to the religion from Imām Aḥmad and he is from those who have narrated a great amount from Imām Aḥmad. *Tarīkh Baghdad* vol. 14, p. 330

83. *Jāmi' al-'Ulūm wal-Ḥikam*, vol. 1, p. 10.

84. *Manāqib al-Imām Aḥmad*, p. 284.

[51] Supplication

ʿAbduraḥmān b. Zādhān[85] said: We prayed and Abū ʿAbdullāh was present and I heard him say:

> O Allāh! Do not busy our hearts with what You have burdened us with. And do not make us with Your provisions as servants (and slaves) to other than You! And do not prevent us from the good which is with You due to the evil that is with us. And do not overwhelm us in what You have prohibited us, and do not deprive us in what You have commanded us. Grant us honour and do not humiliate us. Honour us with obedience (to You) and do not humiliate us with sins (against You).[86]

[52] There is no *Taqlīd* in Creed

Imām Aḥmad said: "From the narrow-mindedness of a man's knowledge is that he blindly follows men in his creed."[87]

[53] The Unknown Remembrance

Isḥāq, the paternal uncle of Aḥmad said: I entered upon Aḥmad and his hand was under his cheek. So I said: "O nephew! What is this (thing causing you) sadness?" So he raised his head and said: "Glad tidings to whoever Allāh makes his *remembrance* unknown (to the people)."[88]

---

85. [EN] He is ʿAbduraḥmān b. Zādhān b. Yazīd b. Makhlad ar-Razi, Abū Īsā. His statements are = mentioned in books such as *Manāqib al-Imām Aḥmad* and *al-Maqṣid al-Arshad*. *Tarīkh Baghdad* vol. 11, p.582.

86. *Tahdhīb al-Kamāl*, vol. 1, p. 464.

87. *Talbīs Iblīs*, vol. 1, p. 101.

88. *Ṭabaqāt al-Ḥanābilah*, vol. 1, no. 12. Meaning that Allāh does not make the person famous whereby everyone knows his affairs all the time which can cause self-amazement, pride, arrogance and wanting to please the people.

[54] Journeying in Pursuit of Knowledge

'Abdurahmān b. Fihm[89] said: I heard Aḥmad b. Ḥanbal say about Egypt where the book *At-Ta'wīl* of Mu'āwiyah b. Ṣāliḥ[90] was present: "If a man came to Egypt and wrote this down and then returned with it, his journey in my opinion would not have been in vain."[91]

[55] Ask About What You Have Been Afflicted With

Aḥmad b. Aṣram[92] said: Aḥmad was asked about a matter pertaining to *al-Li'ān*[93] so he said: "Ask, may Allāh have mercy on you, about what you have been afflicted with."[94]

[56] Chivalry

Imām Aḥmad said: "Chivalry (*al-Futuwwah*) is to leave what you desire when you fear (Allāh)."[95]

---

89. [EN] His name is Al-Husain b. Abdurahman b. Fihm. He was a narrator of Ḥadīth. He memorised many Aḥādīth and was knowledgeable about various sciences such as genealogy and biographies of narrators. *Tarīkh Baghdad* vol. 8, p.657

90. [EN] Mu'āwiyah b. Ṣāliḥ (d. 158 A.H.) was a notable narrator of ḥadīth and the *Qāḍī* of al-Andalus (Spain).

91. An-Nahās, *An-Nāsikh WalMansūkh,* vol. 1, p. 75

92. [EN] He is Aḥmad b Asram b. Khuzaimah b. Abbad. He was severe against the people of innovation in the religion. *Siyar 'Alam An-Nubalā* vol.13, p. 385

93. [TN] *Al-Li'ān* is an oath invoking the curse of Allāh on the lying party during a case where a husband accuses his wife of committing adultery (without four witnesses).

94. *Al-Ādāb ash-Shar'iyyah*, vol. 2, p. 72.

95. *'Uddat as-Ṣābirīn*, vol. 1, p. 27.

[57] The Appearance of Prayer

Aḥmad ar-Raqī[96] said: Abū 'Abdullāh was asked while I was present: "What is the meaning of placing the right hand over the left during the prayer?" So he replied: "It is an act of humility before Allāh ﷻ.[97]

[58] The Frontier

Imām Aḥmad said: "Had these children not been attached to us, leaving this land would have been my wish." It was said: "And where would you choose to live?" He said: "By the frontier."[98]

[59] Critiquing Reporters of *Ḥadīth*

Muḥammad b. Bundār al-Jurjānī[99] said to Aḥmad b. Ḥanbal: "It is difficult on me to say: 'So-and-so is weak' and 'so-and-so is a liar.'" So Aḥmad replied: "If you remain silent, and I remain silent, then when will the ignorant know the difference between the sound and weak?"[100]

[60] He Whose Reward is Upon Allāh

'Abdullāh b. Aḥmad said: I said to my father one day: "Indeed a man came

---

96. [EN] He is Aḥmad b. Yahya b. Hayan ar-Raqi. His statements are mentioned in books such as *Manāqib al-Imām Aḥmad* and *al-Maqṣid al-Arshad.*

97. *Ṭabaqāt al-Ḥanābilah*, vol. 1, p. 84.

98. *Iḥyā' 'Ulūm al-Dīn*, vol. 4, p. 355. [TN] The frontier (*ath-Thugūr*) is a general reference to a seaport in any one of the fortified coastal territories in the Muslim empire.

99. [EN] He is Muḥammad b. Bundār as-Sabbak al-Jurjānī. His statements are mentioned in books such as *Manāqib al-Imām Aḥmad* and *al-Maqṣid al-Arshad.*

100. *Al-Asrār al-Marfū'ah Fīl Akhbār al-Mawḍū'ah,* p. 80; edited by Muḥammad Luṭfī al-Ṣibāgh, published by al-Maktab al-Islāmī.

to Faḍl al-Anmāṭī and said: 'Give me a discharge (*ḥull*).'"[101] [Faḍl] replied: "I have never discharged anyone ever!'" ['Abdullāh] said: So Aḥmad smiled. So when some days went by, he said:

> O my son! I passed this *āyah*:
>
> ﴿ فَمَنْ عَفَا وَأَصْلَحَ فَأَجْرُهُ عَلَى اللَّهِ ﴾
>
> "So whosoever pardons and reconciles, then his reward is upon Allāh." [Quran, 40]
>
> Then I looked at its *Tafsīr* and found this: when it is the Day of Judgement, a caller will call out: "No one stand except those whose reward is upon Allāh!" And none will stand except for those who pardoned. So I have discharged the deceased one[102] from striking me.

Then he started saying: "And it is not for any man that Allāh should punish someone because of him!"[103]

[61] Action for Allāh?

A man asked Imām Aḥmad: "Did you seek knowledge for (the sake of) Allāh?" So he replied: "This is a strict condition! Rather, [Allāh] made a thing beloved to me so I gathered it."[104]

[62] Speech Regarding *Al-Wara'*

Abū Bakr al-Marwazī said: I heard Aḥmad b. Ḥanbal mentioning the characteristics of those who practise *al-Wara'* and he said: "I ask Allāh that

---

101. [TN] In another version of this same story, the man asked Faḍl to discharge (or exonerate) him if he failed to support him. Consult Ibn Mufliḥ, *Al-Ādāb ash-Shar'iyyah* vol. 1 p. 120-121.

102. A reference to the man who used to beat (or whip) Aḥmad during the *Miḥnah*.

103. *Tahdhīb al-Kamāl*, vol. 1, p. 463.

104. *Al-Bidāyah wa 'l-Nihāyah*, vol. 10, p. 330.

He does not hate us. How far are we from these people!"[105]

[63] Imām ash-Shāfiʿī

Muḥammad b. Mājah al-Qazwīnī[106] said: One day Yaḥyā b. Maʿīn went to Aḥmad b. Ḥanbal, and while he was with him, ash-Shāfiʿī passed by on his mule. So Aḥmad leapt up and he gave Salām to [ash-Shāfiʿī] and followed him. Then [Aḥmad] slowed down and Yaḥyā was sitting all the while. So when [Aḥmad] came (back), Yaḥyā said: "O Abū ʿAbdillāh! Why did you do this?" So Aḥmad said: "Leave this matter about yourself ! If you desire *Fiqh*, then cling to the mule's tail!"[107]

And Aḥmad said: "I did not know about the ḥadīth abrogating (*Nāsikh*) and its abrogated (*Mansūkh*) until I sat with ash-Shāfiʿī."[108]

[64] When Greed Sets In

Imām Aḥmad said: "It is required on the slave (of Allāh) to accept provision after despair and not to accept it if greed precedes it."[109]

---

105. *Manāqib al-Imām Aḥmad*, p. 277.

106. [EN] He is Abū Abdillah Muḥammad b. Yazīd b. Mājah ar-Rib'i al-Qizwini. The famous author of Sunan Ibn Mājah. *Siyar 'Alam An-Nubalā* vol. 13, p.278

107. *Ḥilyat al-Awliyā'*, vol. 9, p. 99.

108. *Tārīkh Ibn al-Wardī*, vol. 1, p. 206.

109. *Dhail Ṭabaqāt al-Ḥanābilah,* vol. 1, p. 305. This is the case with what is presented to a person of gifts or donations; so if he was presented with something that his self was looking forward to, he should not accept it; As for when he does not yearn for it, or does not expect it, then there is no obstruction (from taking it), as indicated in the Prophet's ﷺ saying to ʿUmar ؓ: "If there comes to you anything from this wealth and you are neither a greedy person (*mushrif*) nor a beggar, then take it, but if not then do not allow yourself to chase it." Agreed Upon (by al-Bukhārī [no. 1473] and Muslim [no. 1045]).

[65] Enjoin *Taqwā*[110] in Your Heart

ʿAlī b. al-Madīnī said: Aḥmad b. Ḥanbal said to me: "Indeed I would really love to accompany you to Makkah, but nothing prevents from that except that I will raise your hopes or you will raise mine!" [ʿAlī] said: And when I bid farewell to him, I said to him: "O Aba ʿAbdillāh! Council me with something?" He said: "Yes. Enjoin *Taqwā* in your heart, and place the hereafter in front of yourself."[111]

[66] It Would Have Depleted

Ṣāliḥ b. Aḥmad b. Ḥanbal said: I visited my father during the term of al-Wāthiq, and Allāh knows what condition we were in, and he had departed to perform ʿAṣr prayers. He had a *labd*[112] that he would sit on which had befallen many years, to the point that it had frayed, and there underneath it was a note which said:

> It has reached me, O Abū ʿAbdillāh, about you being in hardship and that you have a debt hanging over you. So I have presented to you 4,000 dirhams by way of so-and-so, in order to settle your debt and extend it your family. This is neither charity nor Zakah. Indeed it is only something I have inherited from my father.

So I read this note and I placed it back. When he [Aḥmad] entered, I said to him: "My father, what is this note?" And his face went red and he said: "I kept it from you." Then he said: "Take my reply." And he wrote to the man:

> In the Name of Allāh, the all-Merciful, the Giver of Mercy. Your letter has reached me, and we are in good health. As for the debt, then it is to a man who does not burden us. As for our family, then they are blessed, and all praise belongs to Allāh.

---

110. [TN] *At-Taqwā* is having consciousness of Allāh when doing anything through shielding oneself from Allāh's punishment by obeying His commands while hoping for His pleasure, and steering clear of His prohibitions out of fear of His anger.

111. *Tahdhib Hilyat al-Awliyah* vol.3, p. 141

112. *Labd:* a rug made of unwoven wool.

So I went with the letter to the man who had delivered the man's letter. So he said: "Woe to you! If Abū 'Abdillāh accepted this amount, and, for example, cast it into the Tigris river, [the donor] would have been rewarded, because he is not known for doing good deeds!" Then when some time had elapsed, the man's letter was received like before, and the response was returned as before. Then when a year, or a little less, or a little more, had elapsed, we recalled this [to my father] and [Aḥmad] said: "If we had accepted it, it would have depleted."[113]

[67] A Supplication for an Advisor

'Abdullāh b. Aḥmad b. Ḥanbal said: I would often hear my father say: "May Allāh have mercy on Abal Haytham", "May Allāh forgive Abil Haytham" and "May Allāh pardon Abil Haytham." So I said: "My father, who is Abul Haytham?" So he said:

> When I was brought out to be whipped (in public), and my arms were stretched out as a punishment, there was a youth pulling on my thobe from the back. He was saying to me: 'Do you know me?' I said: 'No.' He said: "I am Abul Haytham, the tramp, the thief, the scoundrel! It was recorded in the register of the leader of the believers that I have been struck by eighteen thousand lashes in specific portions. I was patient with this in obedience to the Shaiṭān for sake of the *Dunyā*. So you be patient in obedience to the all-Merciful (Allāh) for the sake of the religion!"

[Aḥmad] said: "Then I was struck with eighteen lashes instead of eighteen thousand, whereupon a servant came out and said: 'The leader of the believers has pardoned him.'"[114]

113. *Tahdhīb Ḥilyat al-Awliyā'*, vol. 3, p. 142. The meaning of Aḥmad's words is that the days would have passed, and it would have only been food and then no food. But the soul remains noble and rich with dignity. It does not extend its hand to any person.

114. *Ṣifat as-Ṣafwah*, vol. 2, p. 229.

[68] The Lightness of the Account

Imām Aḥmad used to love sparseness, seeking thereby a light account (of deeds on the Day of Judgement).[115] Al-Marwazī said: I heard Aba ʿAbdillāh (Aḥmad b. Ḥanbal) say: "Whoever takes less from the *Dunyā* will have little to account for (in the hereafter)."[116]

[69] Adolescence

Imām Aḥmad said: "Nothing resembles adolescence except an object in my sleeve which falls out."[117]

[70] Undertaking Good Initiatives (Deeds)

Imām Aḥmad said: "Every kind of good, give it importance. (Hasten and) Undertake it before something impedes you from it."[118]

[71] Consuming the Lawful

Abū Hafṣ at-Ṭarsūsī said: I went to Abū ʿAbdillāh (Aḥmad b. Ḥanbal) and said: "May Allāh have mercy on you O Aba ʿAbdillāh! What softens the heart?" And he fell silent (for a while); then he raised his head and said: "O my son! By consuming the lawful!" Then I passed by Bishr b. al-Ḥārith and said to him: "O Abū Naṣr! What softens the heart?" And he replied:

﴿ أَلَا بِذِكْرِ اللَّهِ تَطْمَئِنُّ الْقُلُوبُ ﴾

115. *Dhail Ṭabaqāt al-Ḥanābilah*, vol. 1, p. 305.

116. *Manāqib al-Imām Aḥmad*, p. 198.

117. *Manāqib al-Imām Aḥmad*, p. 198. [EN] Meaning: youthfulness slips away very quickly without being able to hold on to it for long.

118. *Manāqib al-Imām Aḥmad*, p. 199.

> Indeed, it is with by the dhikr of Allāh that the hearts find contentment. [Quran, 13:28]

I said: "Indeed I came from the company of Abū 'Abdillāh." So [Bishr] said: "Hey, what did Abū 'Abdullāh say to you?" I replied: "By consuming the lawful." So [Bishr] said: "He conveyed the foundation!" Then I passed by 'Abdul Wahhāb b. Abūl Ḥasan and said: "O Abal Ḥasan! What softens the heart?" And he replied:

﴿ أَلَا بِذِكْرِ اللهِ تَطْمَئِنُّ الْقُلُوبُ ﴾

> Indeed, it is with by the dhikr of Allāh that the hearts find contentment. [Quran, 13:28]

I said: "Indeed I came from the company of Abū 'Abdillāh." And ['AbdulWahhāb's] cheeks turned red out of delight and he said to me: "What did Abū 'Abdullāh say?" I replied: "By consuming the lawful." So ['Abdul Wahhāb] said: "He conveyed to you the essence. He conveyed to you the essence. The foundation is as he said. The foundation is as he said!"[119]

[72] A Good Intention

'Abdullāh b. Aḥmad said: I said to my father one day: "Council me." So he replied: "O my son! Intend good, for indeed you will remain in goodness as long as you intend good."[120]

[73] A Truthful Admonisher

Imām Aḥmad said: "People are in need of a truthful storyteller!"[121]

---

119. *Tahdhīb Ḥilyat al-Awliyā',* vol. 3, p. 144.

120. *Manāqib al-Imām Aḥmad*, p. 200.

121. *Iḥyā' 'Ulūm al-Dīn,* vol. 1, p. 49; Dār al-Khair edition.

[74] The Science of *Kalām*

Imām Aḥmad said: "The Companion of *Kalām* will never prosper. And you barely see a person who explores *Kalām* except that in his heart is a corruption."[122]

[75] You Joke About The Religion!

Aḥmad b. Ḥanbal heard Yaḥyā b. Maʿīn, and the two of them accompanied one another for many years, saying: "Indeed I do not ask anyone for anything, and if Shaiṭān was to gift me something I would surely eat it!" Thereupon Aḥmad shunned [Yaḥyā] until he sought pardon and said: "I was joking." So Aḥmad said: "You joke about the religion? Do you not know that eating is part of the religion? [Allāh] the Most High presented it before righteous actions and said:

$$﴿ كُلُوا مِنَ الطَّيِّبَاتِ وَاعْمَلُوا صَالِحًا ﴾$$

Eat of the pure and lawful things and do righteous deeds. [Qurʾan, 23:51]"[123]

[76] An Imām in Knowledge

Imām Aḥmad said: "Beware of talking about an issue in which you do not have an Imām (preceding you)."[124] Ibn Taymiyyah said: "And his Imām in this issue was Ibn ʿAbbās 🙵."[125]

[77] Knowledge Which Transpires

Yaḥyā b. Maʿīn said to Aḥmad b. Ḥanbal, and he had seen him walking

---

122. *Ibid,* vol. 1, p. 124.

123. *Ibid,* vol. 2, p. 162

124. *Manāqib al-Imām Aḥmad,* p. 178.

125. *Fatāwā Ibn Taymiyyah,* vol. 32, p. 297.

behind the mule of ash-Shāfiʿī: "O Abū ʿAbdillāh! You abandoned the Ḥadīth of Sufyān which is ascending (ʿUluw) and you walk behind the mule of this youngster and hear from him!?" So Aḥmad said to him:

> If you but knew, you would surely have walked on the opposite side. Indeed the knowledge of Sufyān, if the ascension slips by me I will come to know of it through dissension (*Nuzūl*). But the intelligence of this youngster: if it slips by me I will not come to learn it, neither by ascension or dissension![126]

[78] Say: "I have a Watcher Over Me"

Thaʿlab (Aḥmad b. Yaḥyā)[127] said: I loved to see Aḥmad b. Ḥanbal so I went to him. When I visited him, he said: "Who is this?" I replied: "Thaʿlab." So he said: "What do you seek of knowledge?" I replied: "*Al-Qawāfī*[128] and poetry." So he said:

> Write! Then dictate it to me:
>
> *When but a day elapses from time then do not say;*
> *"I am alone" but say "I have a watcher over me."*
> *And do not reckon that Allāh is heedless of even one hour;*
> *Nor that what we hide from Him is unseen.*
> *We are heedless of the days which follow in succession;*
> *Sins which impress upon them are still sins.*
> *So alas! If only Allāh forgives what transpires;*
> *And He permits our repentance so that we may repent.*

---

126. *Iḥyāʾ ʿUlūm al-Dīn,* vol. 1, pp. 191-192. Imām Aḥmad said a great lesson in arranging matters according to priority. The knowledge that is lost at some point in time takes precedence over what is not missed, and this is an important rule to consider the order of priorities in all matters of life. [TN] What I have translated here, for lack of better terms, are two kinds of Aḥādīth: the "ascending" Ḥadīth has fewer narrators thereby making it more prized since it contains less middle men between you and the Prophet ﷺ. In contrast, the "descending" Ḥadīth has more narrators thereby making it less prized since it is more prone to corruption and requires more effort to investigate potential errors.

127. [EN] He was a great grammarian of the Arabic language of his era. *Tarīkh Baghdad* vol. 6, p.448

128. [TN] *Al-Qawāfī* refers to the science of rhyming in Arabic poetry.

If the epoch does not pass in which you are in;
You remain behind in the epoch, and are a stranger.[129]

[79] But all that Remains is Sin and Disgrace

ʿAlī b. Khashram[130] said: I heard Aḥmad say:

Pleasure perishes from those who reached its pick;
Of the unlawful but all that remains is sin and disgrace.
There remain evil outcomes due to their consequences;
There is no pleasure in that which the Fire follows after.[131]

[80] Sincerity

Imām Aḥmad said:

> Sincerity is that your deed, be it an act of worship, or your refrainment from forbidden things, or any type of good deed, or *taqwā*, is purely intended for Allāh, free is He from imperfections. Sincerity is the soul of an action, and an action without a soul is a dead action. Thus Allāh will not accept it, and nor will it deliver from the Fire.[132]

[81] Actions are Based on Intentions

Imām Aḥmad said in explanation of the Prophet's ﷺ saying: "Indeed actions are only by intentions":

> Indeed a matter does not transfer from a habit into an act of

129. *Manāqib al-Imām Aḥmad,* p. 205.

130. [EN] He is ʿAlī b. Khashram b. Abdurahman b. ʿAṭā b. Hilāl al-Marwazī. He was a trustworthy narrator and heard Ḥadīth from notable scholars such as Sufyān b. Uyaynah. A number of scholars took ḥadīth from him such as Muslim, Tirmidhī etc. *Siyar 'Alam an-Nubalā,* vol. 11, p. 553

131. *Manāqib al-Imām Aḥmad,* p. 205.

132. Cited by Ibn ʿAsākir in ʿAbd al-Ghanī al-Daqr, *Aḥmad b. Ḥanbal (Silsilat Aʿlām al-Muslimīn),* p. 268.

> worship except by the intention.[133] The intention is that you present to yourself and your heart that which you bring forward to it, be it an act of worship or any deed; that you do not intend by it except that it is for Allāh alone, and the action is not shared alongside anyone besides Him. Intention and sincerity are one.[134]

[82] *Ar-Riyā'*[135]

Imām Aḥmad said:

> As for *Riyā',* then how few are those who are pure from it. The crawl of *Riyā'* into the heart is more inconspicuous than the crawling of an ant. None overcomes it except those who confirm that there is nothing worthy of worship except Allāh, and that there is none who benefits or harms, and none who gives nor withholds, except for Him, free is He from imperfections.

[83] Asceticism is not Befitting Except by Asceticism

Isḥāq b. Hāni' an-Nīsābūrī[136] said: Abū 'Abdullāh (Aḥmad b. Ḥanbal) said to me: "Rise up early one day and present me [some writing] about asceticism (*az-Zuhd*)."[137] So I went to him early in the day and said to his wife: "Give me a mat and a cushion." So I spread the mat out in the foyer. Then Abū 'Abdullāh came out and he had some books and an inkpot. He looked at the mat and pillow and said: "What is this?" I replied: "It is for you to sit on." So he said: "Pick it up. [Studying] asceticism is not befitting except

133. *Ibid.*

134. *Ibid.*

135. [TN] *Ar-Riyā'* is to commit an action so as to be seen by people and gain their attention, pleasure or validation.

136. [EN] He is Isḥāq b. Ibrahim b. Hāni' an-Nīsābūrī. He had a close and special relationship with Imām Aḥmad. *Tarīkh Baghdad* vol. 7, p. 404

137. *Manāqib al-Imām Aḥmad,* p. 246.

by (practising) asceticism!"[138] So I picked it up and he sat on the ground.[139]

[84] Not Yet

'Abdullāh b. Aḥmad said: When my father was nearing death, I sat with him. He began to sweat and (fall unconscious) then he would regain consciousness. He opened his eyes and indicated with his hand, like this: not yet, not yet. He did this once, then a second time. Then when he was doing it a third time, I said to him: "O my father! What is this? You are doing this continuously during such a time? You sweat (and become unconscious) until we say: "He has passed away." Then you come back (to consciousness) and say: "not yet, not yet." So he said to me: "O my son! You did not understand what I said?" I replied: "No." So he said: "Iblīs, may Allāh curse him, stands by my shoes. He bites at his fingertips while saying to me: 'O Aḥmad! (you have) eluded me !" So I reply: 'Not yet, not yet.' Until I die."[140]

[85] The Foundations of the Religion

Imām Aḥmad said:

> Seventy men among the *Tābiʿīn*[141], Imāms of the Muslims and jurists throughout the lands agreed on the following: that the Sunnah which the Messenger of Allāh ﷺ died upon is: the first of which is contentment with the decree of Allāh, accepting His command, and being patient under His rule. To take what Allāh commanded, and prohibit what He prohibited, and have sincerity in actions for Allāh. To have faith in *al-Qadr*: the good and bad of it. To forsake arguments, debates and controversies about the religion.[142]

---

138. *Ṣifat al-Ṣafwah,* vol. 2, p. 233.

139. *Manāqib al-Imām Aḥmad,* p. 176. [TN] My thanks to Shaykh Turkmānī for claryifying the meaning of this incident.

140. *Ṣifat as-Ṣafwah,* vol. 2, p. 233.

141. [TN] *Tābiʿīn*: the direct disciples of the Companions of Prophet Muḥammad ﷺ.

142. *Manāqib al-Imām Aḥmad,* p. 176.

Lessons in Patience and Fortitude

from the *Miḥnah* of Imām Aḥmad b. Ḥanbal

Regarding the *Miḥnah* (inquisition) which bears the name of "the creation of the *Qurʾān*", its origin and reason for that is the Muʿtazilah's creed involved negating the attributes of Allāh, the Most High, and their view that the widespread expression among people that the *Qurʾān* is the "Speech of Allāh", thereby affirming the attribute of speech belongs to Allāh, was that (in reality) the *Qurʾān* is "created."

The Muʿtazilah had a favourable position with the Caliph al-Ma'mūn; they also practised logic and had philosophical proofs which underlined their view and they were able to convince al-Ma'mūn of the same.

During this time the *Miḥnah* began with the removal of anyone from official posts in the government who disagreed. Then this evolved into debates with scholars and experts. Then, into coercing people and whosoever opposed it, persecution, until which time it reached the stage of the execution of any opposition.

In the following pages, I will relate some of the texts which illustrate to us incidents from the *Miḥnah* of Imām Aḥmad and what he underwent because of his stance whereby he refused to say that (i.e. accept the position (that "the Qur'ān is created"). The following is extracted from the book *Tārīkh al-Islām* by adh-Dhahabī, may Allāh the Most High have mercy on him.

Al-Ḥāfiẓ adh-Dhahabī, may Allāh the Most High have mercy on him, stated:

The Muslims remained faithful to the code of the *Salaf* in affirming that the Qur'ān is the speech of Allāh, His inspiration and revelation are, uncreated. This continued until the Muʿtazilah and Jahmiyyah emerged and began talking about the "creation" of the Qur'ān, which they did so discreetly during the reign of (Hārūn) ar-Rashīd.

Muḥammad b. Nūḥ related that Hārūn ar-Rashīd said: "It has reached me that Bishr b. Ghiyāth says the 'Qur'ān is created!' For the sake of Allāh it is incumbent on me that if He grants me victory, I will massacre Bishr!"

Bishr stayed in hiding during the reign of ar-Rashīd and when the latter died, Bishr came out of hiding and began preaching misguidance.

I say: then al-Ma'mūn began looking into *Kalām* and holding discussions with the Mu'tazilah. He continued to promote one man and demote another in relation to calling people to the view of the "creation" of the Qur'ān until his resolve was fixed on this issue during the year in which he died [218 Hijri].

The *Miḥnah* During the Era of al-Ma'mūn

Ṣāliḥ b. Aḥmad b. Ḥanbal states: My father and Muḥammad b. Nūḥ were transported in shackles. We reached Al Anbar (Iraq) alongside them. Abū Bakr al-Aḥwal asked my father: "O Abū 'Abdillāh! If you are exposed to the sword will you comply?" [Aḥmad] replied: "No." Then they were taken away.

I heard my father saying: "We reached ar-Rahba and upon us departing from this place during the dead of the night, a man appeared to us and said: 'Which one of you is Aḥmad b. Ḥanbal?' It was said to him: 'This one.' Then the man said to camel-driver: 'Take it easy!' Then he said (to me): 'Hey! Don't worry! If you are killed here, you will enter paradise!' Then he said (to me) 'I entrust you to Allāh's care!' and he departed."

My father said: "I asked about [this man] and it was said to me: 'This man is from the Arabs of Rabī'ah, he composes poetry in the desert. It is said that he is Jābir b. 'Āmir; good things are said about him.'"

Imām Aḥmad said: "I never heard a statement since this affair took place as powerful as the statement of a bedouin who uttered them at ar-Rahba Ṭawq. He said (to me): 'O Aḥmad! If you are killed because of the truth, you will die a martyr. And if you survive, you will live a praiseworthy life!' Thereupon, my heart was empowered."

Ṣāliḥ b. Aḥmad said: My father said to me: "We arrived at Adhanah, a land close to al-Maṣīṣah, and while were being been transported during the dead of the night, its gate was opened before us and there was a man who stepped forward and said: "Glad tidings! The man has died!" i.e. al-Ma'mūn." My father said: "And I had been supplicating to Allāh that I would not meet him [al-Ma'mūn]."

The *Miḥnah* During the Era of Al-Muʿtaṣim

Ṣāliḥ said: When my father and Muḥammad b. Nūḥ arrived at Ṭarsūs, they were put back in their shackles. Then when they reached ar-Raqqah, they were transported by ship. When they arrived at ʿĀnāt, Muḥammad [b. Nūh] passed away. His body was unshackled (from the chains) and my father prayed his funeral prayer.

Abū ʿAbdullāh [Aḥmad b. Ḥanbal] said: "I have never seen someone so young in age or short of knowledge that stood for Allāh's cause than Muḥammad b. Nūḥ. Indeed I hope that his end was a good one. He said to me on that day (i.e. the day he died) something to the effect of: 'O Abū ʿAbdillāh! Allāh! Allāh! Indeed you are not like me. You are a man that people emulate. The people's necks have been brought forward to you to see how you react. So have *Taqwā* of Allāh! And be steadfast in Allāh's cause, or (he said something) similar to this.'"

Ṣāliḥ said: My father was transported to Baghdad in shackles and he was held at al-Yāsiriyyah for a few days. Then he was detained in a rented house near the palace. Next, he was transported after that to the public prison on al-Mawṣiliyyah street. My father said: "I would pray with the prisoners whilst I was in shackles. During Ramaḍān, in the year 219 [Hijri], I was relocated to the home of Isḥāq b. Ibrāhīm."

Aḥmad said: So every day two men were sent to me. One was called Aḥmad b. Rabāḥ and the other Abū Shuʿāyb al-Ḥajjām. They would continue to debate me until they wanted to leave, (then) they would request for an additional chain to be added to my shackles. Both of my legs ended up having four shackles on them each.

Aḥmad said: Then on the third day, one of the men visited me and debated me. I said to him: "What do you say about the knowledge of Allāh?" He replied: "The knowledge of Allāh is created." I said to him: "You have committed disbelief." Thereupon a messenger who was present at the behest of Isḥāq b. Ibrāhīm said: "This (man you are accusing of disbelief) is an envoy of al-Mu'taṣim!" So I responded: "Indeed he has committed disbelief." When it was the fourth night, al-Mu'taṣim sent Bughā, who was referred to as "the senior", over to Isḥāq b. Ibrāhīm and commanded that I be brought to him [the Caliph].

Then I stood before Isḥāq and he said: "O Aḥmad! This is, by Allāh, your life (at stake). [Al-Mu'taṣim] will not merely kill you by the sword. He has vowed that if you do not respond to him positively, he will whip you over and over again and he will execute you at a place where neither the sun or moon can be seen! Didn't Allāh say: 'Indeed We made it an Arabic Qur'ān' [Quran, 43:3]? Can it be made without being created!?" So I responded: "Allāh has also said: 'And We made them like chewed up straw.' [Quran, 105:5] Did Allāh create them [as chewed up straw]?" [Isḥāq] then fell silent.

Then we arrived at a place widely known as the Garden Gate (*bāb al-Bustān*); I was brought out and a riding beast animal was led out and I was placed on it along with the shackles. Nobody was there to hold me and I was almost ejected onto my face several times because of the weight of the shackles.

Then the riding beast was led along with me to al-Mu'taṣim's palace and I was made to enter a quarter and I was put into a house. The door was locked on me and this occurred during the dead of the night. There was not a lamp in the house and I wanted to perform *tayammum* for prayer so I extended my hands. Thereupon I came upon a vessel containing water and a basin next to it. So I performed *Wuḍū'* and prayed.

Then the next day, I removed the drawstring from my trousers and I tied it around my shackles so I could carry them. My trousers leaned to one side (as a result).

Then a messenger belonging to al-Mu'taṣim's envoy arrived and said: "Come." He took my hand, and held me while I carried the drawstring wrapped around my shackles in my other hand, to where [al-Mu'taṣim] was sitting. Ibn Abū Du'ād was present and a great number of his people had gathered.

Al-Mu'taṣim said to me: "Bring him closer. Bring him closer." They continued to bring me forward until I was close to him. Then he said to me: "Sit." So I sat, strained by the shackles which weighed me down.

After a brief moment of silence, I said: "Do you permit me to speak?"

[Al-Mu'taṣim] responded: "Speak."

I said: "To what (thing) did Allāh and His Messenger call to?"

So [Al-Mu'taṣim] paused and then responded: "To the testimony: that there is no deity worthy of worship in truth except Allāh."

So I said: "Well, I testify that there is no deity worthy of worship in truth except Allāh. Then I said: Indeed your grandfather Ibn 'Abbās said: "When the delegation of 'Abd al-Qays arrived at the Messenger of Allāh ﷺ, they asked him about *Imān*. [The Messenger of Allāh ﷺ] replied: "Do you know what *Imān* is? "They said: "Allāh and His Messenger know best. [The Messenger of Allāh ﷺ] said: "[It is] the testimony that there is no deity worthy of worship in truth except Allāh and that Muḥammad is the Messenger of Allāh; to establish the prayer; to give zakat, and to donate one-fifth of the spoils of war.'"

[Ṣāliḥ] said: My father said: he [meaning Al-Mu'taṣim] said: "If I had not found you detained by my predecessor, I would not have brought you here." Then he said: "O 'Abdur-Raḥmān b. Isḥāq! Did I not order you to put an end to the *Miḥnah*?" So I said: "Allāhu Akbar [Allāh is the greatest]! Indeed this will be a tremendous relief for the Muslims." Then [Al-Mu'taṣim] said to them [the people present]: "Debate him. Speak to him. O 'Abdur-Raḥmān! Speak to him!"

Then 'Abdur-Raḥmān said to me: "What do you say about the Qur'ān?"

I responded to him: "What do you say about the knowledge of Allāh?"

So some of them [those present] said to me: "Didn't Allāh the Most High say: 'Allāh created all things' [Quran, 13:16 and 39:62]. And the Qur'ān, is it not a thing?"

I responded: "Allāh the Most High said: 'It [the wind] destroyed everything by the command of its *Rabb*' [Quran, 46:25]. Then did it destroy except whatsoever Allāh wanted it to?"

Then some of them [those present] said: "'Whatever a new reminder comes to them from their *Rabb*' [Quran, 21:2]. Can something new be except something created?"

So I responded: "Allāh said: 'Ṣād. By the Qur'ān, full of reminders.' [Quran, 38:1] Here the reminder is the Qur'ān. Woe to you! Do you not find here *alif* and *lām* (i.e. the definite case)?"

A group of them mentioned the ḥadīth of 'Imrān b. Ḥusayn: "Indeed Allāh created the remembrance."

So I responded: "This is incorrect. We narrate from more than one source: 'Indeed Allāh recorded the remembrance.'"

They sought proof from the ḥadīth of Ibn Mas'ūd: "Allāh did not create Paradise or Hell, nor the heavens or the earth, which is greater than *āyat al-Kursī*."

So I responded: "Indeed the term 'create' only refers here to Paradise, Hell, the heavens and the earth. It does not apply to the Qur'ān."

Then some of them [of those present] recounted the ḥadīth of Khabbāb: "O you! Seek nearness to Allāh with what you are able to do.

For indeed you will not gain nearness to Him with anything more beloved to Him than His speech."

I responded: "This is what it says."

Ṣāliḥ b. Aḥmad said: This made Aḥmad b. Abū Du'ād look at my father with fury. My father said: This one would say this and I would refute him. And that one would say this and I would refute him. And whenever a man among them was defeated, Ibn Abū Du'ād would object and say: "O leader of the believers! He [Aḥmad], by Allāh, is misguided, an innovator!" And So he [al-Mu'taṣim] would respond: "Speak to him. Debate him." So this one would say this and I would refute him. And that one would say this and I would refute him. Then when they were defeated, al-Mu'taṣim said to me: "Woe to you O Aḥmad! What are you saying?"

So I responded: "O leader of the believers! Bring me something from the Book of Allāh or the Sunnah of the Messenger of Allāh (ﷺ) whereby I can repeat it."

Ibn Abū Du'ād said: "You do not say except what is in the Book of Allāh and the Sunnah of His Messenger (ﷺ)?"

So I responded: "As for the interpretations you make, then you know best. As for what I interpret, then it should not be the cause of imprisonment and shackles!"

Abū 'Abdullāh [Aḥmad b. Ḥanbal] said: And they sought proof against me with one matter. It does not empower my heart nor liberate my tongue for me to relate it. They rejected the *Āthār* (narrations). And I did not think they were like this until I heard their words. And they began inviting discord and such-and-such.

Ṣāliḥ b. Aḥmad said: Ibn Abū Du'ād said: "O leader of the believers! That he responds positively to you would be more beloved to me than one hundred thousand dinars" and he called out whatever figure Allāh willed that he would call out.

Al-Mu'taṣim said: "By Allah! If he would respond to me positively, I would set him free with my own hands, and I would lead my army to him and march behind him." Then he said: "O Aḥmad! By Allāh, indeed I am very sympathetic to you. I sympathise to you like I do my own son Hārūn. What do you say?"

So I [Aḥmad] said: "Bring me something from the Book of Allāh or the Sunnah of the Messenger of Allāh (ﷺ)."

Then when the sitting prolonged, [al-Mu'taṣim] became bored and said:

"Everyone get up!" And he held me back alongside 'Abdur-Raḥmān b. Isḥāq so that he could speak to me.

Al-Mu'taṣim said: "Woe to you! Give up! Have you never come to us before?"

'Abdur-Raḥmān b. Isḥāq said: "O leader of the believers! I have known [Aḥmad] for thirty years. He believes that you are to be obeyed and that *jihād* and *ḥajj* is to be performed under you."

[Al-Mu'taṣim] said: "It is said that [Aḥmad] is a great scholar, a scholar of *fiqh*. It wouldn't be a bad thing if he was with me so that he could respond to the people of other religions." Then he said to [Aḥmad]: "Are you familiar with Ṣāliḥ ar-Rashīdī?"

I responded: "I have heard of his name."

[Al-Mu'taṣim] said: "He was my mentor. And he used to sit at that place" and pointed to a corner of the palace, "and I asked him about the Qur'ān. He disagreed with me so I commanded that he be trampled and dragged away." Then he said: "O Aḥmad! Respond to me with something even if it is the least you can do possible so that I can free you with my own hands!"

So I [Aḥmad] said: "Bring me something from the Book of Allāh or the Sunnah of the Messenger of Allāh (ﷺ)."

Then the meeting was prolonged and he stood up. Then I was returned to the place I was imprisoned.

After Maghrib, two men and companions of Ibn Abū Du'ād came to me and stayed overnight. They debated me during their time with me. Then when the time of *Ifṭār* arrived, food was brought out and they urged me the to eat but I refused.

Al-Mu'taṣim sent Ibn Abū Du'ād to watch during some evenings. The latter said: "The leader of the believers says to you: 'What do you say?'" And I responded to this with what I responded to before.

Ibn Abū Du'ād said: "By Allāh! Your name was among the seven which were listed, Yaḥyā b. Ma'in and others, and I rubbed it out. It bothered me that they would arrest you." Then he said: "Indeed the leader of the believers has sworn to whip you repeatedly and discard you into a place in which the sun cannot be seen (a dungeon). And he is saying: 'Indeed if [Aḥmad] responds to me positively I will go to him and free him with my own hands.'" Then he left.

When morning arrived, [al-Mu'taṣim's] messenger arrived, and took me by the hand and took me to him. So [al-Mu'taṣim] said to [the people present in the gathering]: "Debate him. Speak to him." So they debated me and I would refute them. Whenever they would bring forward any words which are not found in the Book and the Sunnah I would say: "I don't know what this is." They would say: "O leader of the believers! Whenever he has a proof against us, he remains firm. And whenever we say something he replies 'I don't know what this is.'" Al-Mu'taṣim replied: "Debate him."

Then a man said: "O Aḥmad! I believe you are relating ḥadīth and pretending to understand."

I replied: "What do you say about [the *āyah*]: 'Allah commands you regarding your children: the share of the male will be twice that of the female' [Quran, 4:11]?"

He replied: "Allāh addressed believers by it specifically."

I said: "What do you say about the murderer and slave?" So the man remained silent.

I only sought proof against them with this (*āyah*) because they would argue by the apparent meanings of the *Qur'ān* whereby one said to me: "I believe you are plagiarising ḥadīth...." So I sought proof with the Qur'ān. And they continued like this until it was nearly mid-day. When [al-Mu'taṣim] became bored, he said [to the people present]: "Stand up" and he kept me and 'Abdur-Raḥmān b. Isḥāq behind, and he continued talking to me.

[Ṣāliḥ] said: Then my father said to me: "Then [al-Mu'taṣim] stood up and entered [his private quarters] and I was returned to my place."

The *Miḥnah* and Subsequent Punishment

[Imām Aḥmad] said: During the third night, I said to myself: "It seems like something is going to happen to me tomorrow." So I said to some of the men beside me who were entrusted (with my imprisonment): "Hand me a rope." So he brought one to me and I wrapped it around my shackles. Then I returned my drawstring around my trousers, worried that if something does happen, that I might become exposed.

Then when the next day arrived, the third day, I was summoned and I entered [al-Mu'taṣim's quarters] into a crowded building. I entered, step by step, while the onlookers bore swords and others bore whips, and other things. There had not been during the previous two days anyone among them.

When I reached to a stop, [al-Mu'taṣim] said: "Sit down." Then he said:

"Debate him. Speak to him." So [those present] began to debate me and one would say this, and I would refute it, while another would say that and I would refute it. My voice raised above their voices.

When the gathering had prolonged, I was taken aside and [al-Mu'taṣim] was left alone with [those present]. Then they were sent aside and I was returned to stand before him. [Al-Mu'taṣim] said: "Woe to you O Aḥmad! Concede to me so that I may free you with my own hands." Thereupon I responded to him as I had done so before.

Then he said to me: "Upon you..." and he mentioned a curse. Then he said: "Take him, drag him out and strip him!"

[Aḥmad] said: Thus I was dragged out and stripped. There had come into my possession a strand from the hair of the Prophet ﷺ which I kept in the sleeve of my shirt. Isḥāq b. Ibrāhīm looked at me and said: "What is this knotted thing in the sleeve of your shirt?"

I responded: A strand from the hair of the Messenger of Allāh ﷺ. Some of the people proceed to rip my shirt off. Then al-Mu'taṣim said: "Dont rip it off." Thus, the shirt was removed from me (without tearing it) and I thought to myself, indeed this prevention from the shirt being ripped was only because of the strand of hair inside of it.

[Aḥmad] said: Al-Mu'taṣim sat on his chair and called for two posts and whips. Two posts were brought forward and my hands were stretched onto them. Some of those present behind me said: "Take hold of the logs with your hands and grip onto them tightly." I did not understand what they meant and ended up dislocating my wrists.

Ṣāliḥ said: My father said: When the whips were brought out, al-Mu'taṣim looked at them and said: "Bring me something else." Then he said to the men charged with doing the whipping: "Proceed." And he made one of the men among them proceed and he whipped me with two lashings. He said on both occasions: "Harder! May Allāh severe your hand!"

After I was whipped 19 times, al-Mu'taṣim stood before me and said: "O Aḥmad! Why are you killing yourself? By Allāh, indeed I am very sympathetic to you!"

[Aḥmad] said: Then 'Ujaifah poked me with the tip of his sword and said: "Do you think that you can win against all of these people?" One [of those present] said: "The caliph is standing right in front of you!" Another said: "O leader of the believers! His blood is on my neck. Kill him!" This caused others to say: "O leader of the believers! You are fasting and you are standing under the sun!"

[Al-Mu'taṣim] said to me: "Woe to you O Aḥmad! What do you say?"

So I replied: "Bring me something from the Book of Allāh or the Sunnah of the Messenger of Allāh (ﷺ) whereby I can repeat it."

Thereupon al-Mu'taṣim returned to his seat and said to those charged with doing the whipping: "Proceed and punish! May Allāh severe your hand!" Then a second man stood up and he proceeded to say: "Woe to you O Aḥmad! Answer me!" Then others turned to me and said: "O Aḥmad! Your Imām is standing before you!" 'Abdur-Raḥmān proceeded to say: "Who among your companions has acted in this matter as you now act!" And al-Mu'taṣim proceeded to say: "Woe to you! Respond to me with something even if it is the least you can do possible so that I can free you with my own hands!"

So I replied: "O leader of the believers! Bring me something from the Book of Allāh."

Then [al-Mu'taṣim] returned and said to those charged with doing the whipping: "Proceed!" So one of them proceeded to whip me with two lashings and then gave up. During this time, [al-Mu'taṣim] was saying: "Harder! May Allāh severe your hand!"

[Ṣāliḥ] said: My father said: Then my senses gave way and I passed out after this. I regained consciousness to find the shackles had been taken off me. A man who was present said to me: "We threw you to the ground head first. We stomped on your back and trampled you."

[Ṣāliḥ] said: My father said: I did not even feel this. I was brought *Sawīq* (a meal made of barley) and [those present] said to me: "Drink up and vomit!" So I replied: "I will not break my fast." Then I was transported to the house of Isḥāq b. Ibrāhīm where I attended the *Ẓuhr* prayer. Ibn Samā'ah stepped forward and lead the prayer. When he completed the prayer he turned and said to me: "You prayed while blood was pouring from your thobe?" So I replied: "'Umar prayed while blood spurted out of his wound."

[Ṣāliḥ] said: Then [my father] was freed and returned to his home. And his time in captivity from the time he was arrested and transported to the time he was whipped and released lasted 28 months.

[Ṣāliḥ] said: I begged and tried to reach my father with food and bread during those days but I was not able to.

[Ṣāliḥ] said: A man who was present [with my father] informed me that he was there during the three days they debated [my father] but he did not even make a mistake in grammar. The man said: "And I thought that nobody equals him in bravery and strength of heart."

Ḥanbal said: I heard Abū 'Abdullāh [Aḥmad b. Ḥanbal] say: "My senses departed several times. When they ceased to whip me my senses returned to me. I drooped and fell down when they stopped flogging. This occurred to me several times. I saw [al-Mu'taṣim] sitting under the sun without shade and then he made them stand me up while I heard him saying to Ibn Abū Du'ād: "I have forced this issue with this man!" So [Ibn Abū Du'ād] replied: "O leader of the believers! Indeed [Aḥmad] is a disbeliever, a *Mushrik!* He has committed *Shirk* in various ways!"

Muḥammad b. Abū Samīnah said: "I heard Shābāṣ, the repentant, saying: "I had flogged Aḥmad with 80 lashings. If I had been whipping an elephant, I would have destroyed it!"

Abū Muḥammad aṭ-Ṭafāwī asked Aḥmad: "O Abū 'Abdillāh! Tell me about what they did to you?" [Aḥmad] replied: "When I was flogged, that man with a long beard, i.e. 'Ujaifah, came and hit me with the tip of his sword. I said to myself: 'Relief is near! He will strike my neck and I will finally rest.' Then Ibn Samā'ah said: 'O leader of the believers! Strike his neck and his blood is on my neck!' Ibn Abū Du'ād said: 'O leader of the believers! Don't do it! If [Aḥmad] is executed or dies in your palace, the masses will say [Aḥmad] was patient until he was murdered! They will take him as a leader and become resolute in his stead. Instead, free him for a time, and if he dies outside of your palace the people will doubt about the cause.'"

Al-Mu'taṣim's Fear for Aḥmad's Life

Abū Zur'ah said: Al-Mu'taṣim called Aḥmad b. Ḥanbal's paternal uncle and then said to the people: "Do you know him?" They responded: "Yes, that is Aḥmad b. Ḥanbal." [Al-Mu'taṣim] said: "Look at him. Is he not sound in body?" They replied: "Yes." Had [al-Mu'taṣim] not done this, I fear something would have occurred which he could not have stood against. So when [al-Mu'taṣim] said: "I have returned [Aḥmad] to you sound in body"; the people calmed down and abated.

Ṣāliḥ said: My father was transported back to his home and during the morning, [al-Mu'taṣim] sent to him those who would inspect the wounds and carry out surgery. And they treated [my father] from his wounds. One of them inspected the wounds and said to us: "By Allāh! I have seen someone who has been flogged by a thousand lashings! [However] I have never seen more severe wounds than this. They have been inflicted on him on the front and back." He proceeded to treat him. But [my father's] face was affected by other than the flogging. Then the man remained there treating [my father] until what time Allāh willed.

Then he said: "Indeed this here, I want to cut it. He brought out an iron contraption and proceeded to fasten it onto a piece of flesh with it and he cut it off with a knife. And he [my father] was patient, praising Allāh all the while. Thereafter [my father] recovered. And he continued to feel pain in certain places and the traces of the flogging were visible on his back until the day he died.

I heard my father saying: "By Allāh! Indeed I gave it my all. And I would love to have been saved from this affair, and that it did not happen to me or to others because of me."

Al-Mu'taṣim ordered Isḥāq b. Ibrāhīm that he not stop delivering him news about [my father]. And this happened during the time he settled, according to what was related to us, in al-Iyās. And news reached us that al-Mu'taṣim regretted (his actions) and dropped (his head) into his hands (out of shame) until he felt better.

And Isḥāq, who would inform [al-Mu'taṣim] would come to us every day to know about [my father's] condition until he recovered. And Abū Isḥāq was relieved of his duty by al-Mu'taṣim. I have observed that Allāh says: "Let them pardon and forgive. Do you not love to be forgiven by Allah?" (Quran, 24:22) And the Prophet ﷺ ordered Abū Bakr to pardon in the story of Misṭaḥ. Abū 'Abdullāh [Aḥmad b. Ḥanbal] said: "To pardon is more virtuous,. And it would not benefit you if a Muslim was punished because of you!"

The *Miḥnah* During the Era of al-Wāthiq

Ḥanbal said: Abū 'Abdullāh [Aḥmad b. Ḥanbal] continued to attend the *Jumu'ah* and congregational prayers after he recovered from his wounds. And he would deliver fatwas and narrate ḥadīth until al-Mu'taṣim passed away and was replaced by his son al-Wāthiq (in the year 227 Hijri).

Al-Wāthiq set forth whatever he wanted of the *Miḥnah* and he gravitated towards Ibn Abū Du'ād and his companions.

Then when the affair intensified over the people of Baghdad, and the judges of the *Miḥnah* emerged, Abū 'Abdullāh [Aḥmad b. Ḥanbal] would attend the *Jumu'ah* and repeat the prayer when he would return home saying, "The *Jumu'ah* is to be attended due to its virtue, but the prayer is repeated if prayed behind someone who says this kind of thing (i.e. that the Qur'ān is 'created')."

A delegation visited Abū 'Abdullāh [Aḥmad b. Ḥanbal] and said: "This affair (i.e. the *Miḥnah*) has spread and worsened! Now we fear that it will intensify." They mentioned Ibn Abū Du'ād was determined to command all teachers to instruct children in Qur'ān schools that the Qūr'ān is such-and-such (i.e. "created"). [The delegation said] "Therefore, we do not accept [al-Wāthiq's] leadership." So [Aḥmad b. Ḥanbal] forbade them from proceeding (to revolt) and he debated them.[143]

While we experienced the days of al-Wāthiq, Ya'qūb once visited during the night with a letter from Isḥāq b. Ibrāhīm for Abū 'Abdullāh [Aḥmad b. Ḥanbal] which read: The leader says: "The leader of the believers has stated about you: Do not gather with anyone nor reside on any land or city in which I am present. Go wherever else on Allāh's earth you please."

So Aḥmad [b. Ḥanbal] went into hiding for the remainder of al-Wāthiq's life in other than his own home. Then he returned to his home after some months after news circulated about [al-Wāthiq's] impeding death. But he remained in hiding in his own home and he would not exit leave (his home) for the prayer or for other than that until al-Wāthiq finally passed away (232 Hijri).

During The Era of al-Mutawakkil

Ḥanbal said: Ja'far al-Mutawakkil assumed leadership and Allāh made the Sunnah manifest and the people found comfort. Abū 'Abdullah [Aḥmad b. Ḥanbal] would narrate ḥadīth to us and his companions during the era of al-Mutawakkil. I heard [Aḥmad] saying: "The people are not more in need

143. The delegation planned to revolt against Wāthiq so Imām Aḥmad forbade them and convinced them not to.

of ḥadīth and knowledge than the people during our times!"

Then it was conveyed to al-Mutawakkil that Aḥmad b. Ḥanbal is waiting on an 'Alawī in his home and that he wishes to bring him forward and give him the oath of allegiance. All the while we had no knowledge of this.

While we were asleep one night during the summer, we heard an uproar. We looked out and saw the house of Abu 'Abdullāh [Aḥmad b. Ḥanbal] on fire so we rushed out.

We came upon Abu 'Abdullāh [Aḥmad] sitting in his *Izār* between Muẓẓafar b. al-Kalbī, a messenger, and a group of men. The messenger read out a letter from al-Mutawakkil: "It has been related to the leader of the believers that you are harbouring an 'Alawī. You are waiting on him in order to pay your oath of allegiance to him and bring him forward." The letter kept going. Then Muẓẓafir said: "What do you say?"

Aḥmad [b. Ḥanbal] said: "I do not know anything about this. Indeed I only believe in hearing and obeying [al-Mutawakkil] during my times of ease and hardship, in my favour or not, even if preference is given over me. Indeed I only supplicate to Allāh during the night and day for [al-Mutawakkil] to remain upright and successful."

So Ibn al-Kalbī said: "The leader of the believers has ordered me and said: 'Upturn the home of Abū 'Abdullāh [Aḥmad], the sewer cellar[144] (below his home), the rooms and roofs. Ransack the boxes of books, interrogate. Quiz the women and probe the home.'"

But they did not find anything nor did they notice anything suspicious. This was relayed back to al-Mutawakkil.

Thereafter [al-Mutawakkil] took a laudable position and knew that Abū 'Abdullāh had been slandered.

After some days, while we were seated by the door of [Aḥmad's] house, Ya'qūb, who was one of al-Mutawakkil's ushers, came upon us. He sought permission to join Abū 'Abdullāh [Aḥmad b. Ḥanbal]. He came forward and some of his servants carried *badrah*[145] while he carried a letter from al-Mutawakkil.

He proceeded to read it to Abū 'Abdullāh: "The leader of the believers is satisfied by the innocence of your domain; he presents to you this wealth to aid you." But [Aḥmad] declined it and said: "I have no need for it."

[Ya'qūb] said: "O Abū 'Abdullāh! Accept what you have been ordered

144. An underground excavation that has no exit.

145. A type of bag containing 10,000 dirhams which is given as a gift.

by the leader of the believers! Indeed this is a good thing for you in his stead. Accept it and do not refuse it. Indeed if you reject it, I fear that [al-Mutawakkil] will think ill of you."

Thereupon, [Aḥmad] accepted it and said: "O Abū 'Alī! Take this *badrah.*"

But Abū 'Abdullāh [Aḥmad] was unable to sleep. He called his son 'Abdullāh and experienced some pain for having taken the wealth. His son eased him and said: "Not until you wake up and you consider your choice. Right now it is night time and the people are in their homes."

Then when the morning arrived, [Aḥmad] beckoned a group of noblemen and they arrived, and his two sons Ṣāliḥ and 'Abdullāh were also present. [Aḥmad] made them write down the names of sheltered and righteous peoples in Baghdad and Kufa whom they knew were needy.

Then [Aḥmad] divided all of the wealth, into fifties, hundreds and two hundreds. Thereafter not a single dirham remained in his pursebag. Then he gifted the purse bag to the poor.[146]

Indeed once the period of persecution had ceased, under the reign of al-Mutawakkil began a new chapter whereby he sought friendship with Aḥmad b. Ḥanbal and his proximity. But every attempt ended up in failure. Imām Aḥmad assigned himself a great number of self-sacrifices. He did not accept anything from [al-Mutawakkil] or anyone other than him, so much so that nothing was eaten from the table-spread.

Al-Mutawakkil tried to tend to Imām Aḥmad and confer on him honours. But this attention caused great anguish on Imām Aḥmad, to the extent that he cried, "I was safe from them (the rulers) for sixty years, now when I have reached the end of my life, I am trialled by them! By Allāh! I had wished for death during the affair which occurred, the trial of al-Mu'taṣim, and indeed I wish for death again. That is because this is a trial related to the *Dunyā* and that was a trial related to the hereafter."

[Aḥmad] clasped his hands together saying: "If my soul was in my hands I would have sent it forward (to death)." Then he released his hands.

When al-Mutawakkil was convinced of the futility that of his attempts at friendship with Imām Aḥmad was empty, he left [Aḥmad] alone and his affair. At this point the issue of the *Miḥnah* came to an end after it had ran for 14 years. Imām Aḥmad remained firm during it with the steadfastness of truthful believers.[147]

---

146. Here ends the extract from *Tārīkh ul-Islām* by adh-Dhahabī.

147. Consult the biography by al-Banna in *al-Fatḥ ar-Rabbānī.*

May Allāh have mercy on Imām Aḥmad and make him among those on whom He favours: the prophets, truthful believers, martyrs and righteous!

[*Āmīn*!]

Printed in Great Britain
by Amazon

41459083R00037